Golf Whiz

The Young Prodigy

Written by:
Mark Satorre

Dedication

"To my cherished children, whose inspiration fuels my storytelling."

"To my son, whose passion for his favorite game sparked the creation of this adventure book."

"For my daughter, whose melodies on the piano are the sweetest symphonies to my ears."

Table of Contents

Prologue

In a small town where the days seem endless and the streets echo the silence of the empty playground, a young boy named Charlie discovers a hidden passion that will change his life forever. As the world grapples with the challenges of a global pandemic, the boy finds himself confined to the four walls of his home, yearning for the freedom of the outdoors and the joy of playing with his friends. Little does he know that amid the uncertainty and isolation, a new chapter is about to unfold – one that will lead him down a path of discovery, determination, and unwavering dedication.

It all began during the unprecedented Covid lockdown, when Charlie's world seemed to shrink with each passing day. His love for sports life has been put on hold, leaving a void in his heart that only the thrill of competition could fill. Fate has a different plan for Charlie, one that will introduce him to a game unlike any he had ever played before.

Join us on a journey through the winding fairways of Charlie's life, as he embarks on a remarkable adventure that tests his skills, ignite his passion, and, ultimately, shapes his destiny. From the tranquil serenity of a local driving range to the grandeur of a professional golf course, Charlie's story is a testament to the power of perseverance, the bond between a father and son, and the endless possibilities that await those who dare to dream.

This is a tale of courage, resilience, and the transformative magic of a simple game called golf.

Chapter 1
How it all began

In a small town lived a young boy named Charlie. He had a great fascination for sports. He played soccer, basketball, and even tried his hand at baseball, but nothing really clicked. During the Covid lockdown, Charlie spent most of his days stuck at home, unable to go out and play with his friends. He missed the sun on his face and the wind in his hair. Charlie had been cooped up in his house for what seemed like an eternity.

He missed his friends, his school, and his extracurricular activities. His parents were anxious, looking for ways to keep him occupied and active. One day, his mother and father decided to take him to the local golf driving range after the lockdown had been lifted.

Chapter 2
The driving range

Charlie had never played golf before, and he wasn't sure what to expect. He was hesitant at first, but as soon as he saw the lush green fairways and the neatly trimmed grass, he felt a new sense of peace and calm.

As his parents took turns hitting balls, Charlie watched with curiosity. Swinging their clubs, his parents looked like they were having a lot of fun. He asked if he could try, and his parents happily handed him a golf club.

"Hey, let me try!" insists Charlie, excited.

As he took his first swing, he was hooked. It felt like living in a dream. The sound of the club hitting the ball was music to his ears, and the ball soaring through the air was like nothing he had ever experienced.

"Wow. That was fun. Can I do it again?" he asked eagerly.

At first, Charlie's swings were clumsy and uncoordinated, but with a little guidance from his parents, he soon found his rhythm. He was amazed at how far the ball flew when he hit it just right. He had never felt so exhilarated in his young life.

"Did you see the ball fly? Like a bird on the wing, huh?" Charlie offered.

Charlie spent the entire day at the driving range, practicing his swing and trying to hit the ball farther and farther. From that day on, Charlie couldn't get enough of golf. He begged his parents to take him to the driving range every weekend, and he spent every spare moment practicing in the backyard.

"Mom, Dad…is it time to go yet? asked Charlie on a regular basis.

As he got better, surprisingly, Charlie began to dream of becoming a professional golfer. He watched videos of famous golfers like Tiger Woods and Rory McIlroy, studying their swings and learning everything he could about the game.

Chapter 3
At the real course

One day, Charlie's parents surprised him with a trip to a golf course. He was so excited to play on a real course for the first time, but he was a bit nervous. The course was long and intimidating, and he wasn't sure if he was ready.

"I can't believe I am here. What a dream!" exclaimed the boy.

As soon as he stepped onto the first tee box, Charlie took a deep breath, lined up his shot, and swung the club. The ball soared through the air, landing right in the middle of the fairway. Charlie couldn't believe it. He had never hit a shot like that at the driving range.

"Did I really do that!" he cried.

As he made his way around the course, the sun was shining, the birds were singing, and he was doing what he now loved most in the world. He knew that golf was his game. He started to watch golf tournaments on TV and dream of playing like the pros one day.

As soon as he was back at school, he begged his parents to sign him up for golf lessons. Charlie's parents could see the excitement in his eyes and encouraged him to keep playing. They took him to the course every chance they got. Charlie quickly fell in love with golf and began to improve rapidly.

"Golf is for me. I know it's my game," insisted Charlie.

Charlie knew that he needed to work hard if he wanted to improve; however, he found it challenging to practice alone. Dad stepped in to help. Charlie's dad had always supported his son's dreams, and he offered to play with him every weekend.

Chapter 4
Charlie and his dad

Charlie was thrilled and excited to have his dad as a regular golf partner. However, he would often lose to his dad, which was discouraging. But Charlie's dad always encouraged him to keep practicing and told him that practice makes perfect.

"Dad, I may not win now, but I'll keep practicing until I can beat you one day!" chirped the boy.

To make the game more interesting, his dad suggested a friendly competition. Charlie would have to eat a sandwich filled with mayonnaise and mustard if he loses, and since Charlie hated the idea, it was an excellent incentive to win. To further motivate Charlie, his dad proposed a deal to buy him the newest game console when he wins. Charlie was ecstatic and practiced even harder.

"I dare you, Dad, to beat me," claimed Charlie.

The day came when Charlie broke his personal best score. His dad gave him money for a gaming console as promised in the deal. Charlie was thrilled. He continued to work hard. Week after week, Charlie and his dad would play golf together. It was not about winning or losing. It was about spending quality time and enjoying their mutual passion for the sport. Charlie was grateful to have a dad who believed in him and supported him every step of the way.

"Let's go, Dad," was a regular refrain, as often as Charlie could utter it.

He started to win more often; eventually, he was consistently beating his dad. Charlie's confidence grew, and he became even more passionate about the sport. He began to compete in local junior golf tournaments and found that he had a natural talent for the game. His parents were overjoyed to see him happy and thriving. But Charlie knew he could only go so far with his dad as a coach.

Chapter 5
Charlie gets a coach

Charlie's parents could see the excitement in his eyes and encouraged him to keep playing. Having watched golf tutorials online, Charlie's Dad remembered a particular video and contacted a coach named Chris. When they arrived at the golf course to meet him, they were greeted by a warm and welcoming young man. He immediately put Charlie at ease and began to teach him the basics of golf. Chris was patient and encouraging.

"Chris, I'm glad you're here to help Charlie with his swing. He needs all the help he can get," Dad said.

Over the next few weeks, Charlie worked tirelessly with Chris to improve his technique. Charlie felt like he was making progress with every swing. He practiced every day. Plus, he watched countless videos of golf strategy and tips from online tutorial videos. He even got his own set of clubs and often went to the driving range to practice. His parents could see his passion and dedication. Their son excelled even at the beginner level.

One day, Chris noticed that Charlie's swing was stuck and decided to challenge him. That means his club is behind him during his swing.

"Charlie," the coach said, "I want you to improve your game this summer. I believe in you and know you can do it."

Charlie was hesitant at first, knowing it would take hard work and dedication. But he accepted the challenge.

"I am happy to comply. Working hard is what it takes!" said Charlie.

He was determined to become a better golfer. Every day that summer, Charlie practiced tirelessly. He now headed to the course every morning. His dad would drive him and drop him. He would push his golf cart in the heat and work on his putting, chipping, and golf swing.

At first, Charlie struggled. His shots weren't consistent, and he became frustrated. But he refused to give up and kept practicing every day. As the weeks went by, Charlie noticed a difference in his game. His shots became more accurate, and he was hitting the ball farther. He was beginning to feel more confident and excited about his skill. Chris had been the answer for sure.

"I'm getting there, slowly but surely," Charlie insisted, while assessing his obvious improvement.

His coach cheerfully acknowledged his statement. "You have done your homework, my boy. Bravo for the good results."

After a long and challenging summer, Charlie's hard work paid off. He had improved his game significantly and became a better golfer. He was proud of himself and grateful for his coach's challenge.

Chapter 6
Tournament time

One day, Charlie learned that a local junior golf tournament was to be held in his town. He immediately signed up and was thrilled when his parents agreed to watch him play. The day of the tournament arrived; Charlie was both excited and nervous. He put on his lucky golf shirt and headed to the course with his parents. The weather was perfect, with a gentle breeze and a clear blue sky.

"Is this not the best day in my life?" shrieked Charlie, beyond excited.

As Charlie walked to the first tee, he felt his heart pounding. He took a deep breath, closed his eyes, and imagined the perfect shot. When he opened his eyes, he saw Mom and Dad standing at the side of the course, smiling and cheering him on.

"Mom, Dad…I'm am so happy you are with me on my big day," blurted Charlie.

"We wouldn't miss it," they replied.

"You bring me love, luck, and support. I appreciate it," concluded the boy.

"You are our pride and joy," they professed.

Charlie took his stance, swung his driver club, and sent the ball flying down the fairway. It landed right in the middle, just where he wanted it. He felt a wave of confidence wash over him as he made his way to the ball.

Over the next few holes, Charlie played some of the best golf of his life. He sank a long putt for a birdie, chipped in from the rough for another birdie, and made several more great shots. His parents were watching every move and shouting encouragement at every turn.

As the round went on, Charlie grew more and more confident. He knew he had a chance to win the tournament if he kept playing well. But he also knew that there were other talented players in the tournament, and he couldn't afford to make mistakes.

"Hey, gang. Are you watching? Did you see that!" It feels so amazing," Charlie quipped.

"You bet," shouted Mom and Dad with glee. They were so proud of their golf whiz; the young prodigy.

Finally, the group reached the 18th hole, and Charlie was in a tie for first place. He looked over at his parents, who were beaming with pride. He knew that he couldn't let them down.

Charlie took his final shot and watched as the ball soared through the air. It landed on the green, just a few feet from the hole. He sank the long putt for another birdie and looked up to see his parents running toward him, tears in their eyes.

"You did it, Charlie!" Dad exclaimed. "You won the tournament!"

"Yes….I did," Charlie choked out, breathless.

"Great job, kid! We are so proud of you!" his parents said, in chorus.

Charlie hugged his parents tightly and smiled. He felt a sense of pride and accomplishment that he had never felt before. He had achieved his dream of playing in a golf tournament and had won it with his parents by his side.

As Charlie grew better, he saw the possibility of one day becoming a professional golfer. It was a long shot, but he was willing to put in the work. His parents encouraging him to follow his dream of playing in the biggest tournaments in the world.

Eventually, Charlie was offered a scholarship to play golf in college. He accepted and continued to practice and play, honing his skills and perfecting his game. After a year in college, Charlie turned professional and played on the tour for several years. He was respected by his peers for his dedication and skill on the course. At last, he was a pro!

Chapter 7
Life as a pro

After this initial success, Charlie approached every game with newfound confidence and determination. He now knew that hard work and dedication are the keys to success, and he was ready to take on any new challenge. With his love of golf, he would never stop pushing himself to be the best he could be.

Eventually, Charlie entered his first major golf tournament. He was nervous but also excited to show off his skills. Thanks to Chris' guidance and tutelage, Charlie played one of the best games of his life. He was focused, calm, and precise, and ended up winning the tournament.

Years passed and Charlie continued to enter tournaments and won them all. He made it to golf world championship and placed in the top ten. Charlie's life had changed forever. With the help of his coach, Charlie had discovered his true passion and became a star on the golf course.

He had been fortunate to have had the opportunity to pursue his dreams, and he wanted to help others do the same. But it was at the driving range where Charlie really shone as a student of the game and then role model. He would finish his bucket of golf balls, one after the other, hitting them with precision and power. His driver and irons were his favorite clubs, and he knew how to use them to their full potential.

Charlie continued to play, passing on his knowledge and passion for the game to the next generation of young golfers. Charlie retired from professional golf and returned to the local course where he had first learned to play. He was a different person now, older and wiser, but he still loved the game just as much as when he was a boy.

Years later, Charlie would look back on that first day at the driving range as the moment that changed his life. Golf had given him a sense of purpose and a passion he would carry with him for the rest of his life. He had his parents to thank for introducing him to a game that had brought him so much joy.

One summer day, as he watched the sun set over the course, Charlie felt a sense of peace and contentment. He knew that he had lived a good life, one filled with the love of family and the joy of playing the game he loved.